Albert the Octopus Accountant

For my grandfather,
who taught me how to balance a checkbook.
(But did not have eight arms.)

YOU ALREADY KNOW WHAT AN OCTOPUS IS...
...BUT DO YOU KNOW WHAT AN ACCOUNTANT IS?

AN ACCOUNTANT IS SOMEONE WHO HELPS PEOPLE WITH THEIR MONEY. SOMETIMES HE HELPS BUSINESSES, AND SOMETIMES HE HELPS FAMILIES.

BUT WHAT HE REALLY LOVES TO DO...

WHAT IS MONEY?

MONEY IS WHAT YOU
USE TO TRADE FOR
THE THINGS YOU
NEED AND WANT.

THE FOOD YOU EAT COSTS MONEY..
THE CLOTHES YOU WEAR COST MONEY...

EVEN YOUR TOYS AND THE PRESENTS YOU GET ON HOLIDAYS COST MONEY!

BUT HOW DO FAMILIES GET AND USE MONEY? AND WHY IS IT IMPORTANT FOR YOU TO KNOW?

ALBERT IS HERE TO TELL YOU!

THERE ARE LOTS OF WAYS TO GET MONEY BUT MOST OF THE ADULTS IN YOUR LIFE GET IT BY WORKING JOBS.

THAT'S WORK YOU DO FOR SOMEONE ELSE.

THERE ARE ALMOST AS MANY TYPES OF JOBS AS THERE ARE FISH IN THE SEA!

WHAT JOBS DO YOU SEE ON THIS PAGE?

abcd
1234

WHEN YOU DO A JOB, YOU GET PAID MONEY.
SOMETIMES IT'S A LITTLE. SOMETIMES IT'S A LOT.
SOMETIMES JOBS LAST ONLY A FEW DAYS. BUT SOME
PEOPLE CAN WORK AT THE SAME JOB FOR MANY YEARS!

ALL JOBS ARE DIFFERENT!

WHAT DIFFERENT KINDS OF MONEY DO YOU SEE ON THIS PAGE?

MOST MONEY IS KEPT IN A BANK.
A BANK IS A PLACE THAT HOLDS MONEY
FOR A LOT OF PEOPLE AT ONE TIME.

WHEN YOUR FAMILY NEEDS TO USE THEIR MONEY THEY CAN GO TO THE BANK AND TAKE SOME.

OR THEY USE SOMETHING CALLED A DEBIT CARD. THAT'S A PIECE OF PLASTIC THAT HAS YOUR MONEY ON IT.

ALBERT ALWAYS USES HIS DEBIT CARD AT THE STORE TO BUY HIS FAVORITE PENCILS. WHAT DO YOU LIKE TO BUY AT THE STORE?

BUT IT'S NOT A GOOD IDEA TO GO TO THE STORE AND SPEND ALL YOUR MONEY ON WHATEVER YOU WANT.

A FAMILY HAS TO THINK ABOUT WHAT THEY NEED NOW AND WHAT THEY NEED LATER.

A PLAN FOR YOUR MONEY IS CALLED A BUDGET. SOME MONEY YOU WILL SPEND RIGHT AWAY AND SOME MONEY YOU WILL PUT AWAY FOR THINGS YOU NEED LATER.

FOOD IS SOMETHING YOU NEED EVERY DAY.

SO SOME MONEY BUYS THAT NOW.

BUT SOMETIMES YOU DON'T HAVE ENOUGH MONEY RIGHT NOW FOR SOMETHING YOU WANT. SOME THINGS COST A LOT OF MONEY - LIKE CARS, OR COMPUTERS, OR HOUSES.

SOMETIMES YOU ONLY HAVE TO SAVE MONEY FOR A FEW MONTHS TO BUY WHAT YOU WANT. SOMETIMES YOU HAVE TO SAVE MONEY FOR YEARS! SAVING MONEY IS HARD WORK BUT IMPORTANT.

ALBERT IS SAVING HIS MONEY TO BUY
A VERY FANCY CALCULATOR. WHAT IS
YOUR FAMILY SAVING MONEY FOR?

ALWAYS HELP WITH CHORES.
YOUR FAMILY SPENDS A LOT
OF TIME AT WORK AND STILL
HAS TO COME HOME TO
COOK YOU DINNER AND
CLEAN YOUR CLOTHES.

AND ALWAYS THANK THEM FOR THE PRESENTS YOU GET
ON HOLIDAYS. THEY HAD TO WORK HARD
FOR THE MONEY IT TOOK TO BUY THEM FOR YOU.

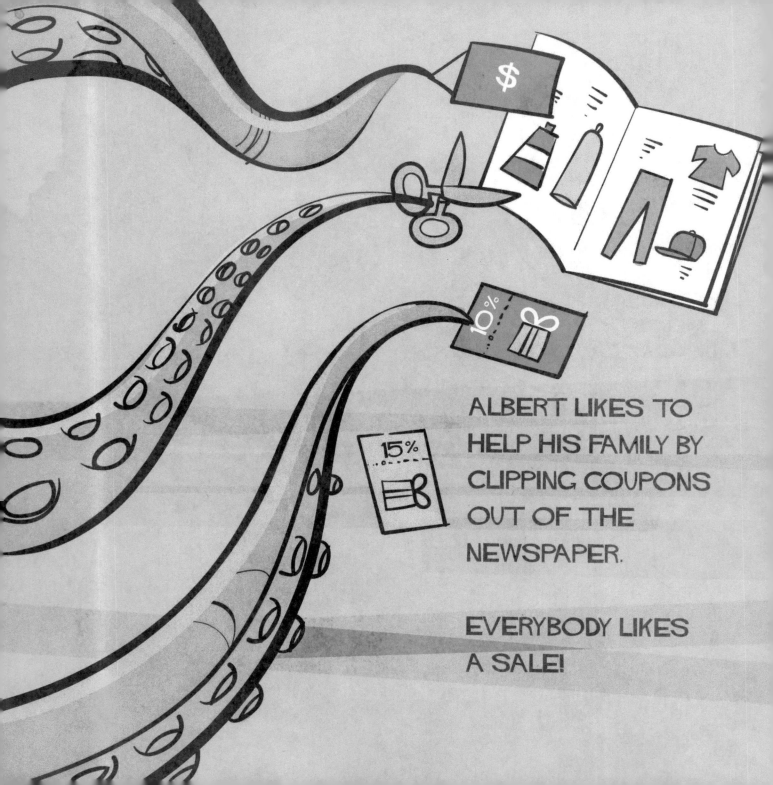

ALBERT LIKES TO HELP HIS FAMILY BY CLIPPING COUPONS OUT OF THE NEWSPAPER.

EVERYBODY LIKES A SALE!

REMEMBER THAT EVERY FAMILY IS DIFFERENT! THEY ALL HAVE DIFFERENT JOBS AND NEED TO BUY DIFFERENT THINGS.

SOMEDAY YOU MIGHT HAVE YOUR OWN FAMILY, YOUR OWN JOB, AND YOUR OWN MONEY!

BUT IF YOU EVER HAVE TROUBLE
AND DON'T KNOW WHAT TO DO,
JUST GO OUT AND FIND A SMART
AND HELPFUL OCTOPUS!

Hi! I'm Lily Verlin.

Author of Albert the Octopus Accountant. I started this series when a friend of mine told me how hard it was for her to find books for kids about money and finance. Sure, there were a lot of books for older kids and plenty of books for adults on how to raise financially literate children, but there weren't a lot of options for younger children who were just setting out on their reading journey.

How do we start to raise our kids to understand money long before they're out in the world and making their own? We need to start much earlier with the basics.

Like me, my friend grew up in a household that didn't talk about money. Some still treat it as a taboo subject for "adults only." But that attitude about money really does us such a disservice. For me, it wasn't until I was 18 and working my second job that my Grandfather sat me down and taught me how to balance my checkbook for the first time. Even then, I still struggled with money until I was 25 and got interested in budgeting and more conscious of my financial situation. I can't help but think that if I'd started talking about money at a much younger age I could have avoided a lot of heartache, debt, and overdraft fees!

So let's work to build a nation of budget-conscious kids eager to read, learn, and save!

For more information on upcoming projects, visit LilyVerlin.com

Help support a self-published author and review your purchase on Amazon.